NOWRUZ
COLORING BOOK

THIS COLORING BOOK BELONGS TO:

....

....

SABZEH

SPROUTS

SAMANU

PUDDING

SENJED

OLEASTER

SERKEH

VINEGAR

SEEB

APPLE

SEER

GARLIC

SOMAQ

SONBOL

HYACINTH

SEKKEH

COIN

SAAT

CLOCK

TOKHM-E MORG RANGI

AYINA

MIRROR

SHEM'A

CANDLE

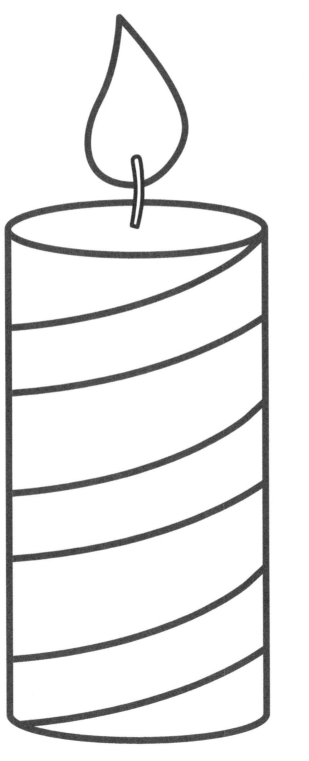

MAAHI-YE QIRMIZ

GOLDFISH

KETAAB

BOOK

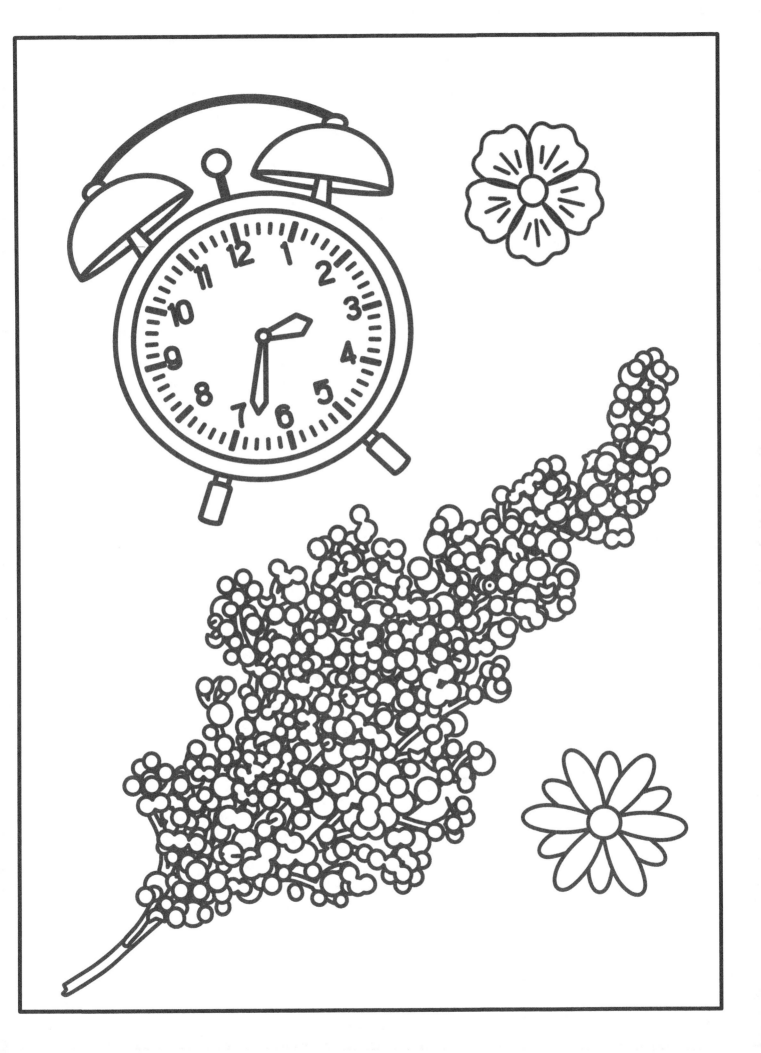

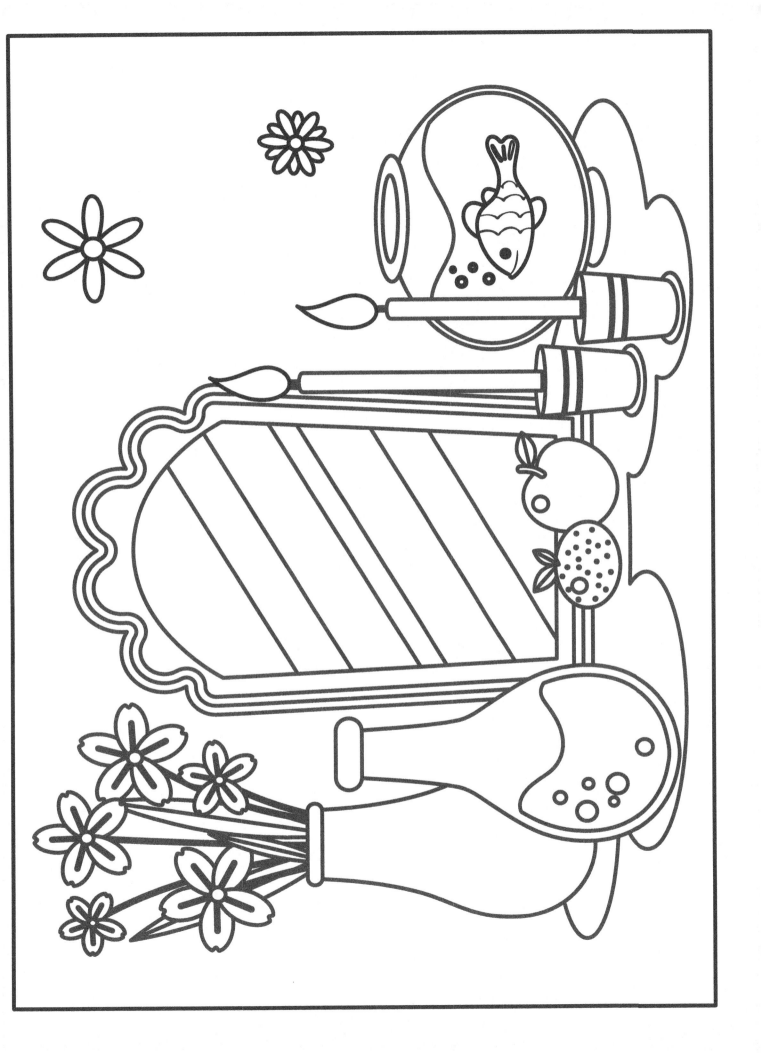

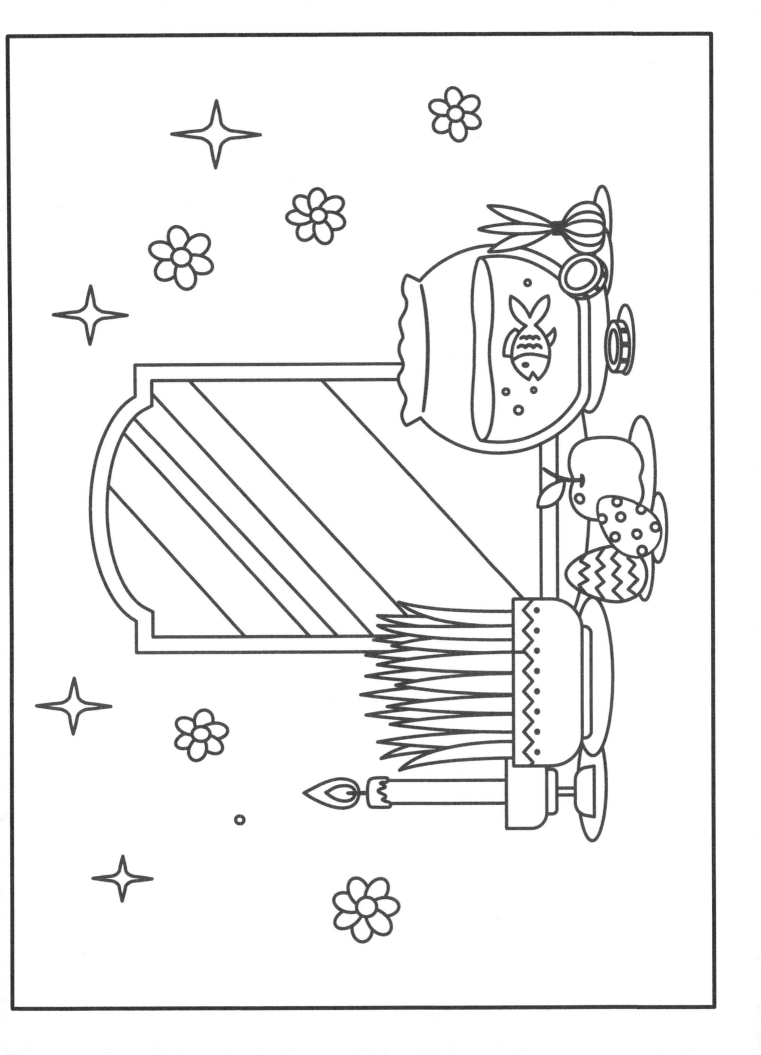

WE REALLY HOPE YOUR LOVED ONE
ENJOYED OUR COLORING BOOK.

THANK YOU FOR CHOOSING US AND
FEEL FREE TO LIVE US A COMMENT.

HAPPY NOWRUZ FROM I-KIDDO PRESS!

Made in the USA
Las Vegas, NV
16 March 2024

87314005R00044